P9-BJB-384

Westminster Public Library
3705 W 112th Ave
Westminster, CO 80031
www.westminsterlibrary.org

DISCARD

Zoom In on
Stars of Music

Beyoncé

Jennifer Strand

abdopublishing.com

Published by Abdo Zoom™, PO Box 398166, Minneapolis, Minnesota 55439. Copyright © 2017 by Abdo Consulting Group, Inc. International copyrights reserved in all countries. No part of this book may be reproduced in any form without written permission from the publisher. Abdo Zoom™ is a trademark and logo of Abdo Consulting Group, Inc.

Printed in the United States of America, North Mankato, Minnesota
092016
012017

THIS BOOK CONTAINS RECYCLED MATERIALS

Cover Photo: Chris Pizzello/AP Images
Interior Photos: Chris Pizzello/AP Images, 1, 15; Frank Micelotta/Invision for Parkwood Entertainment/AP images, 5, 16–17; Jorg Hackemann/Shutterstock Images, 6; Seth Poppel/Yearbook Library, 7; Jim Smeal/WireImage/ Getty Images, 8; Bill Greenblatt/Liaison/Getty Images, 9; Frank Micelotta/ImageDirect/Getty Images, 10; Rose Hartman/Archive Photos/Getty Images, 11; Everett Collection/Shutterstock Images, 12, 14; New Line/Photofest, 13; Shutterstock Images, 17; Featureflash Photo Agency/Shutterstock Images, 18; 13th Witness/Invision for Parkwood Entertainment/AP Images, 19

Editor: Emily Temple
Series Designer: Madeline Berger
Art Direction: Dorothy Toth

Publisher's Cataloging-in-Publication Data
Names: Strand, Jennifer, author.
Title: Beyoncé / by Jennifer Strand.
Description: Minneapolis, MN : Abdo Zoom, 2017. | Series: Stars of music | Includes bibliographical references and index.
Identifiers: LCCN 2016948676 | ISBN 9781680799170 (lib. bdg.) | ISBN 9781624025037 (ebook) | 9781624025594 (Read-to-me ebook)
Subjects: LCSH: Beyoncé, 1981- --Juvenile literature. | Rhythm and blues musician--United States--Biography--Juvenile literature. | Singers--United States--Biography--Juvenile literature.
Classification: DDC 782.42164092 [B]--dc23
LC record available at http://lccn.loc.gov/2016948676

Table of Contents

Introduction

Beyoncé Knowles is a famous singer and actress. She has made award-winning **albums**. She has also starred in successful movies.

Early Life

Beyoncé was born on September 4, 1981. She grew up in Texas. She was a gifted singer.

She won her first talent
competition when she was seven.

Beyoncé formed a music group
with three other girls.

The group was called Destiny's Child.

Their music was very **popular**.
But they split up in 2005.

Superstar

Beyoncé made a **solo** album in 2003. It was a hit.

She also acted in movies.
She became a huge star.

Beyoncé continued making new albums.

She won many **Grammy Awards.**

In 2013 Beyoncé released a surprise album.

It sold more than 800,000 copies in one weekend.

Then she released a film
and album in 2016.

It was a surprise, too. Once again Beyoncé showed she was a global superstar.

Beyoncé

Born: September 4, 1981

Birthplace: Houston, Texas

Husband: Jay-Z

Known For: Beyoncé is a famous singer and actress. She has won several Grammy Awards.

Key  Dates

1981: Beyoncé Giselle Knowles is born on September 4.

1998: Destiny's Child releases its first album.

2003: Beyoncé releases her first solo album, *Dangerously in Love*.

2005: Destiny's Child separates. They perform a farewell tour.

2013: Beyoncé releases her fifth solo album.

2016: Beyoncé releases the film and album *Lemonade*.

Glossary

album - a collection of music.

competition - a contest between two or more persons or groups.

Grammy Award - an important honor given out each year for music. There are many Grammy Awards.

popular - liked by many people.

released - made available to the public.

solo - a performance by a single person.

Booklinks

For more information
on **Beyoncé**, please visit
booklinks.abdopublishing.com

Zoom In on Biographies!

Learn even more with the Abdo Zoom
Biographies database. Check out
abdozoom.com for more information.

Index